THEN AND THERE SERIES
GENERAL EDITOR
MARJORIE REEVES, MA., Ph.D

A Medieval King Governs

MARJORIE REEVES

LONGMAN

LONGMAN GROUP LIMITED
London
Associated companies, branches and representatives throughout the world.

© Longman Group Ltd 1970

First published 1970
ISBN 0 582 20466 6

Photoset and printed in Malta by St Paul's Press, Ltd

ACKNOWLEDGEMENTS

For permission to reproduce photographs we are grateful to the following: British Museum, pages 3, 33, 47, 62, 63 and 69; Bodleian Library filmstrip of St Cuthbert, pages 6, 61 *above*, 74 and 76; Caisse National des Monuments Historiques, pages 77 and 78; Corpus Christi College, Cambridge, pages 64 and 65 *above*; The Governing Body of Christ Church, Oxford, page 5 *above*; the author and publisher of *Court Life under the Plantagenets*, Hubert Hall, London, 1901, pages 8, 17, 24, 36 and 38; The Metropolitan Museum of Art, Cloisters Collection, page 68; The Pierpont Morgan Library, M638 ff. 17 and 27v, pages 14 and 65 *below*; the Ministry of Public Buildings and Works, page 30; the Phaidon Press and the author for the photograph on page 13 from *The Bayeux Tapestry*, edited by Sir Frank Stenton; the Public Record Office, pages 5 *below*, 25, 42 and 43; Société des Anciens Textes Français, pages 55, 71, 72 and 73, from M. Paul Meyer; edition of *La Vie de Saint Thomas*; the author and publisher of Stotharp, *Monumental Effigies of Great Britain*, 1817, page 48; Trinity College, Cambridge, page 35; University Library, Cambridge, page 2; and University of London, Warburg Institute, page 11. We are also grateful to the following authors and publishers for permission to base maps on theirs: page 20 from E. Lodge, *Gascony under English Rule* Methuen, 1926, page 39 from Charles Johnson, *Dialogus de Scaccario*, Nelson's Medieval Classics; pages 58–9 from G. Unwin, *Guilds and companies of London* Methuen, 1908; and page 66 from a map by Miss M. B. Honeybourne in the Historical Association leaflet Nos. 93, 94; *Norman London*.

Contents

To the Reader

Kings in history have often tried to make themselves famous, and they have sought fame in many different ways. Some, like Alexander the Great, set out to be great conquerors. Others, like Solomon, wanted to be remembered for their wisdom, or for their laws, like Justinian. King Alfred the Great hoped people would remember him for his good deeds and King Louis IX of France wanted to be the King who would reconquer the Holy Land and Jerusalem from the Turks. Several medieval English Kings were famous because they managed the country successfully. This did not mean that they were always good rulers and never cruel or unjust. But they did try to make rules and to see that people kept them. They aimed at stopping powerful nobles from bullying weaker people and they were often successful. In doing this they thought up a lot of good ideas about government which we used in this country for many centuries. This book is about one of these Kings – Henry II. If you want to see some of his ways of governing for yourself, go to the Public Record Office in London and ask to see some tally-sticks and pipe-rolls. You will find out in this book what these were.

I King Henry II of England

Medieval kings are often drawn holding a large sword, and many people think that they governed like that – by waving a big sword and smiting down anyone who got in their way. It is true that sometimes they did do this, but governing a kingdom was in fact a good deal more complicated.

Take King Henry II of England, for instance. He was a young man of twenty-one when he was crowned in 1154. His mother, Queen Matilda, had fought a rival, King Stephen, for years to get that crown. While they fought, barons and knights had taken the law into their own hands and – in some parts of England at least – had done as they liked. They had built castles, captured castles from other barons and put their enemies into dungeons without trial. In the Then and There book, 'The Medieval Castle', you can read some stories of these lawless men.

What was the young new king going to do? Of course he was determined to make all men obey the king's law. But no one at that time was quite sure just what the king's law was, for it was not written down in one big law-book. At his coronation King Henry had to take the Coronation Oath, that is, he made three solemn promises: to make good laws, to protect the weak and to punish evil-doers. In making these promises, people said, the king had put himself under God and the Law, so that he was not free to do just what he liked. On the other hand, at his coronation also the king had been solemnly anointed and set above all other men, so that his commands must be obeyed. Some people said: 'The will of the Prince has the force of law', which meant that the king's wishes were law. Thus there were

1

The coronation of a medieval king

two almost contradictory ideas about the king's power. What people really wanted was a king who would use all his own will-power and force to stamp out evil-doers and make everyone keep good laws. Was Henry II going to be that sort of king?

Several chroniclers tell us what he looked like and what kind of a man the barons found when they rode to his court. He was a powerful young man, with strong arms and broad chest. He had reddish hair, keen grey eyes and a freckled face. As he grew older, he would have got fat, only he took care to eat and drink little and get a lot of exercise. He was always on the go, never resting, perpetually rushing off somewhere else. He never seemed to sit down except on a horse. His great passion was for hunting and hawking. He would be up at crack of dawn, riding to the chase in forest or over mountain-top.

His servants found, however, that he did not forget to govern. He was so full of energy that he could do all the business of government before he set off to hunt, ride all day, and then at night make his exhausted courtiers stand round discussing problems when they wanted to sleep. What he liked to do was to plan his journeys to take him to good hunting places, like Woodstock or Clarendon, and then settle important questions of government in the hunting-lodge there. He was certainly not a hunting king with no brains. He had a mind like a *gimlet* and was always asking questions, especially of the educated men, the clerks in his court who could give him new knowledge. Learned men dedicated books to him and he could speak and write elegantly himself. He could not bear doing nothing: if he had to sit and listen in church he was fidgeting all the time, drawing pictures or whispering to his courtiers. He was one of the most energetic kings England has ever had.

But King Henry had a temper. Those grey eyes could flash with fire if someone angered him.

A king and a bishop receive a warning

3

He could be kind to people who begged favours and very pleasant when things went well. But he was fierce to anyone who opposed him and if he once hated someone, could hardly ever bring himself to like him again. Unfortunately he quarrelled bitterly with his family. He married a beautiful and brilliant wife, Eleanor of Aquitaine, who brought him many lands in France. They had three daughters and six sons. Two died young, but Henry, Richard, Geoffrey and John grew up to be energetic, hot-tempered young men, like their father. They wanted lands and power, and quarrelled with Henry because they did not think he gave them enough of either. Their mother, Queen Eleanor, took their side and egged them on. We shall hear more about these family quarrels later.

Henry's main palace was at Westminster. Edward the Con-fessor, last king of England before the Normans came, had first built a palace there to be near Westminster Abbey which he was also building. Then William II (William Rufus, Henry's great uncle) built the great Westminster Hall which we still have – although much altered. By Henry's time many other buildings had sprung up and the palace sprawled over a wide space, a maze of courtyards, gardens, towers and houses of all shapes. The gardens went right down to the river Thames on one side; on the other, the palace was enclosed in walls.

Suppose we imagine ourselves going in through one of the guarded gates. Inside we see a wide courtyard full of people bustling about on many jobs. Huntsmen are polishing spears and horns or feeding shaggy wolf-hounds; *falconers* sit with their hooded *falcons* letting them bask in the sun; grooms are exercising the great heavy horses called *chargers* or the smaller ones, *palfreys* which are ridden by ladies. But other things are going on besides preparations for sport. A king's messenger clatters in on a steaming horse bringing an urgent letter for the king. Others ride out on royal business. King's sergeaunts and men-at-arms hurry to and fro, for Henry cannot bear to be kept waiting. Above all, there is an endless procession of clerks carrying parchment rolls or *writs* with seals dangling from them or bags of money or just their quill pens and ink-

A royal writ in the time of Henry's mother, Matilda

horns. These are the men who do the king's business in government.

The palace at Westminster is not just the place where the king lives and amuses himself. It is also the place where the work of government goes on. If we cross the courtyard to a new part of the palace, overlooking the river, and climb a winding stone stair, we reach a low, stone-walled room with a heavy oak table and iron-bound oak chests against the walls. This is where the Treasurer does his work. We shall be visiting him for a longer

Chest in which Domesday Book was kept

time later. In other rooms the writing-clerks sit surrounded by parchment rolls of all kinds, as they write out with great flourishing strokes the *charters* in which the king makes gifts of land to those he favours.

The king's chamber is not far away. Here the king receives those who come with *petitions* and discusses business with his councillors. The walls of the room are hung with deep crimson canvas, while here and there the royal arms make a brilliant splash of colour. The floor is covered with rushes and at one end of the room there is a splendid chair for the king, with boars' heads carved in ivory at the end of each arm and scarlet cloth on the seat. Crowds of courtiers, barons and knights, bishops and monks, stand around gossiping, telling stories and quarrelling until the king comes from his inner room. On the day of our imaginary visit he is wearing a long tunic of red cloth embroidered with gold flowers and a short cloak of reddish-chocolate colour, fastened on the right shoulder with a brooch. He wears tight-fitting crimson hose and green boots decorated with gold; round his waist is a belt of gold. He means to go hawking, but first he walks all round, talking to various people, settling problems and quarrels, sometimes arguing about the law with his cleverest servants, for Henry loves a good dispute.

Some of his courtiers enjoy working for a king who uses his brains. Peter of Blois, a learned scholar says: 'With the king of

Courtiers talking

England it is school every day, constant conversation of the best scholars and discussion of problems.' But the gay ones find it boring and you would probably see some stifled yawns as Henry talks. When the great *troubadour* Bertran de Born, visited Henry's court he did not like it at all: 'There was no joking' he complained, 'no laughter, no giving of presents.'

This was not really true. At least, Henry had good story-tellers at his court. One of these was Walter Map. He was always entertaining the courtiers with stories and wrote down a huge collection of them in a book called 'Courtiers' Trifles'. I think he liked ghost stories and marvels best. He tells one tale of a Welshman who watched by a lake in the brilliant moonlight for three nights in succession. He saw a band of beautiful women dancing in his oatfield but when he pursued them they sank into the lake. On the fourth night, however, he managed to catch one of them. She promised to be a good wife so long as he did not strike her with his bridle rein. They lived happily for many years, but one day the husband forgot the warning and struck her with his rein. His wife disappeared. Walter Map also tells us about Nicholas Pipe, a real Merman, and many other marvels, which most of his listeners believed completely.

2 *The King's Household*

King Henry has a small army of ministers, servants and soldiers around him. All these together are called the king's household. There are all sorts of people, from important barons and bishops to humble huntsmen and washerwomen. The top people help Henry to govern but they are partly his personal servants too, for the affairs of government and of running the household are very much mixed up. We know how the king's household was organised when Henry's grandfather, King

A king at dinner—not a grand feast

Henry I, died, because someone wrote an account of the *Domus Regis* then – that is the Latin for Home of the King. The second Henry made some changes but probably the general arrangements were much the same.

First of all, because food and drink are so important, we will look at the departments of the Pantry, Larder, Kitchen and Buttery. Imagine what it must have been like to cater for a family of two or three hundred perpetually moving about from castle to castle and county to county. Obviously you had to have large stocks of bread, meat and wine laid in at various places all over the kingdom. (Remember that there was no deep freeze.) The king's chief bakers were busy all the time, buying corn and flour to stock up the castles, king's huntsmen were organising hunts to keep the larders full of game, and king's butlers were filling up the cellars with wine which they bought at fairs or from foreign merchants whose ships came in to Southampton and Bristol. Under these chief men there was a whole horde of humbler servants cooks and bakers, scullions and cupbearers, carters and the like.

The men in charge of all this business had to be able to count and do simple arithmetic, for they had to make an account of all they bought and how they *dispensed* it, that is, gave out food and drink to be consumed. The king was very sharp on accounts. He wanted a check kept on everything. Once when a large number of chestnuts arrived for roasting he wanted to know afterwards what had happened to the sacks in which they came. When brass pots were bought for his kitchen the cost was carefully put down in his accounts. So in the king's household there was a master-dispenser of bread, a master-dispenser of the larder, a chief cook, a master butler and so on. Their wages and allowances were carefully laid down. For instance, the master-dispenser of bread got 2s a day if he ate indoors and 2s 10d if he ate out, besides an allowance of wine and twenty-four candle-ends and some other things. The wages of other chief dispensers were similar and under them the rest of the servants' wages were carefully graded. Over all the separate departments there was one chief man, the steward or *dapifer*. 9

The servants of the king's Chamber, his bedroom, looked after his clothes, his treasure, his bed and his personal comfort. Wherever he went the king's bed went with him, and also a large chest in which his rich robes, jewels, treasures and important documents were stored. Especially important was the stock of money which was carried with the royal treasures. (All payments were made in cash, there were no cheques.) So the servants of the Chamber had to be particularly good and trustworthy. There were a bearer of the king's bed, various *chamberlains*, the king's tailor, the king's washerwoman, the *usher* of the Chamber, the man who looked after the candles, the man who stoked the fire and so on. There was also a special servant to look after the king's bath and dry his clothes when he got wet. This servant received 4*d* every time the king took a bath. In charge of them all, with a watchful eye on the king's treasure and money, was the master-chamberlain.

Then there were the *marshals* of the king and all the men who ran his stables and arranged his sport. Their duty was to look after the royal *studs* of horses all over the country, as well as the packs of hounds, the hawks and the falcons. They had to see that the animals and birds were in good shape, that there was good hunting whenever and wherever the king wanted it, and that the larder was well supplied with meat to eat at once or to salt down. They also saw that the carts for carrying the royal baggage round England were in good running order. There was a marshal of the stables, a chief hunstman, and perhaps a master marshal over the whole lot. Under them were many special kinds of servants. These are only some of them: knight-huntsmen, ordinary huntsmen, fewterers (keepers of greyhounds), wolf-hunters, falconers, horn-blowers, archers, trumpeters.

Lastly there was the king's Chapel, in some ways the most important department. Wherever the king went, the priests and clerks of his chapel accompanied him, for each day they said the service called Mass for the king. They carried everything needed for the service with them, sometimes even the altar, and so there were special horses and carts belonging to the chapel. The chaplain was in charge of the services, but many of the chapel clerks now served the king in another way. They were educated men, able to write good Latin, and previous kings had got into the habit of using the chapel clerks to write their letters (called writs) and draw up the charters in which kings gave land or other gifts to their subjects. By Henry II's time there was a regular writing department, with a master of the writing chamber in charge of all the clerks (we should call them secretaries). The master would see that the clerks had parchment and sealing-wax all ready for use, since the king might want them suddenly. He would not sign his letters or charters; instead they would be stamped with his seal. Two tags of parchment were left hanging at the bottom of the document, a blob of sealing-wax stuck the two ends together, and while this wax was soft the king's Great Seal was impressed on it. This was really the king's signature, so it was extremely important that the great seal should not be put on a false letter or a gift the king had not made. Thus a most important officer was put

Henry II's Great Seal. Notice what he holds in his hands

B*

in charge of the Great Seal which he must keep always with him: this was the *chancellor*. He was the head of the whole writing department. By the end of Henry I's reign, he had become so important that he was paid 5*s* a day and was given wine, a large wax candle and forty candle-ends. Henry II probably raised his wages.

The steward, the chamberlain, the marshal and the chancellor had been first of all concerned with the king's household and personal affairs. They still were, but governing the country had become mixed in with their work. If the king was going to war, the steward's staff would be busy buying provisions for the army and the Marshal's staff would be collecting transport. The chamberlain received newly-minted money and helped to find fresh supplies of cash when the king was short. The chancellor sealed the king's orders and despatched messengers to carry them out. Above all, the king needed advice as he journeyed round the country, for there were many problems to settle. So his chief servants, as well as some of his barons and bishops, were his advisers and helpers in government.

3 The King on his Travels

We paid a visit to Henry in his palace at Westminster when the place was full of people coming and going on the king's business. But for much of the time Westminster was half empty, for the king would not be there. Henry governed his lands by riding continuously round them from castle to castle and manor to manor. Remember that there was no telephone and no quick transport. If you wanted to know what was going on in the country, you had to ride there to see. Henry liked to keep his eye on his chief servants in the counties, who were called *sheriffs*; also on his barons and the keepers of his castles. So he kept on the move, hearing disputes, punishing criminals, granting favours, hunting and hawking, all in the same day.

Wherever Henry went his household (or most of it) went too. There were probably several hundred people perpetually trundling round England with the king – that is, when they were not all setting sail for France. What a job it must have been

Hawking

getting them all packed up and off to the next place! If you had met them riding north, say, from St Albans or Northampton, it would have seemed like an army on the move. First, and a long way ahead, would be the king and his courtiers on fine prancing horses with red leather harness and rich saddles. Henry might be trying out a new hawk on the way. Once he was presented with a magnificent snow-white hawk from Norway which fought a most exciting battle in the air with a crane. But just when the hawk was winning, the crane struck him in the throat and he fell to earth like a stone. Some way behind the king and his energetic younger courtiers came the more elderly of Henry's ministers – the chancellor with the Great Seal, the *Justiciar* and two or three justices, the steward of the household, a bishop or two, the priests of the chapel and others. Some would look weary and disgruntled as they jolted over rough stones or struggled through deep mud. It was hard work doing the king's business while moving on each day! Then a long way further back still, came all the baggage carts that so often got stuck in the mud. There was an enormous long-cart which carried the king's treasure. The

Baggage wagon. What is it carrying?

kitchen needed a couple of smaller carts called *carettes* and the Buttery and Larder several more. With these came a troop of pack-horses carrying the king's armour, the vessels and vestments for the chapel, a blacksmith's forge for shoeing the horses and all the baggage of the courtiers. Imagine the noise: whips cracking, wheels creaking, carters swearing, and swarms of servants shouting as they ran along beside the groaning carts. Twenty miles a day was all that could be managed, if those on foot were to keep up easily.

As he rode along, Henry thought about punishing criminals and bringing peace, as well as about hawks and hunting. He would discuss what needed to be done with his clever bishops and the clerks that knew the law. In the year 1166 he rode round the south-west and came to his hunting-lodge at Clarendon near Salisbury. There, with the advice of his councillors, he decided to make a special set of orders about catching and punishing criminals. This is called the *Assize* of Clarendon and it deals with thieves, robbers and murderers. There was no police force then and the problem of catching and holding these desperate men was a serious one. Each village had the duty of chasing after them in the hue and cry. But the villagers would often stop after a few miles and go back to their work in the fields. King Henry now ordered his sheriffs in every county, with their servants, to follow hard after suspected criminals, not stopping at county boundaries or at any obstacle. They were even to go charging into the special parts belonging to barons, if need be. A still greater problem was to get the criminals properly tried and punished when they had been caught. Someone had to accuse them in court and it was risky for one person to do this – can you see why? There was already another way of accusation: by a whole group of people, usually twelve of them. They had to be trusted men of the neighbourhood who knew what had been going on. In the Assize of Clarendon Henry ordered that this way of bringing thieves, robbers and murderers to justice was to be used everywhere. The sheriff in a local court was to hear the first accusation and then twelve men from the district called the *hundred* were to make a solemn accusation before a royal judge sent by the king to try the criminals.

But there was still another problem: how to prove whether the accused man was guilty or not. This was a very serious matter. Even today, with all our modern aids to finding out the truth, we make mistakes and occasionally innocent men are condemned as guilty. In the twelfth century people felt it was too grave a matter to let human beings give a verdict of guilty or innocent, especially when the punishment was often death. Only God, they said, really knew the truth; so they tried to appeal to God's judgment in a curious kind of trial: ordeal by water or by red-hot iron. In the ordeal by water the accused man was bound and thrown into a pool. If he sank he was declared innocent because the water had received him; if he floated, he was guilty because the water had rejected him. In the second kind of ordeal, the accused man had to carry a piece of red-hot iron a certain distance. If his burnt hand festered, he was guilty. Sometimes this ordeal was done by plunging a bandaged arm into boiling water: if the arm showed signs of scalding after three days, then the man was guilty.

These ways of trying accused persons had been going on for a long time but in King Henry's time people were beginning to doubt if the ordeal was anything but a piece of luck. Henry himself suspected that it did not tell any truth about guilt or innocence and that the twelve neighbours' accusation was a much safer guide. He dared not stop the ordeal altogether, but in his new Clarendon rules he ordered that a man accused by twelve neighbours – even though he got through the ordeal successfully and so was apparently innocent – was to *abjure the realm*, that is, go right out of the country, because the neighbours probably knew best.

When these rules had all been decided, Henry's clerks got busy writing them out in Latin, and soon the king's messengers were galloping in all directions to take them to the sheriffs in all the counties. The king meanwhile was deep in Clarendon forest hunting, not criminals, but the red deer.

16   Henry had another problem to think about. As he rode

The king hunting. Can you see any rabbits?

through the country people came to him with complaints and petitions. They came to Westminster, too, seeking remedies for their wrongs. One of the commonest complaints came from landowners who said that such-and-such a knight or baron had come with armed men and turned them out of their land by force. This was called *disseisin*: the wronged landowner was disseised of his land. Very often he was not as strong as his opponent and it was difficult to get justice. The usual way had been to go to his lord's court and claim the land as his. But his enemy might be a friend of the lord (sometimes even the lord himself), and in any case he might find himself in for trial by battle, that is, having to fight a kind of duel for his land. Henry did not like trial by battle any more than he liked trial by ordeal. Too many big bullies were able, through trial by battle, to get away with deeds of violence like turning peaceful men out of their lawful possessions. They had done it during the reign of King Stephen and they were still trying it on with King Henry.

Henry was determined to stop it. He consulted his lawyers and justices and they came up with an answer to the problem which had occasionally been tried before. It was a different way of trying the case, called the Assize of Novel Disseisin. Henry sent out orders about this and other matters of justice from Northampton in 1176, when he was riding to the north. 17

This assize said that the knight who had been disseised could go to Westminster and, by paying a fee, get the king's clerks to send a writ to the sheriff. This ordered the sheriff to collect twelve trustworthy neighbours who knew the truth and summon them to a court before a royal judge. There, after taking a solemn oath to tell the truth, they had to answer one important question: Has A (the man who was complaining) been newly disseised – turned off his land – by B? If they answered Yes, then B must immediately return the land to A. This seems to us a simple and obvious way of doing justice. It was not so simple in the twelfth century, especially as people were often afraid of the consequences if they told the truth in a lord's court. The king's court had more power: it could punish people who told lies and protect those who told the truth – at least generally, if not always. So the king invited landowners to come to his court for settling this particular sort of trouble (and others as well), because they could get better justice by the verdict of their neighbours than by trial by battle. Henry really managed to kill three birds with this stone: he satisfied complaining people, he stopped the big bullies having it all their own way and he put money in his own money-bags.

But this might not be the end of the matter. Suppose the man who had turned the other one out really thought he had a right to the land? When he was forced to return it he would be very discontented, so he would probably try to go to law himself by claiming the land as his by right. What will the other man (who has been given back the land and is peacefully sitting on it) do now? Henry's lawyers have thought out a new remedy for him. He can ask for the grand assize. This prevents him from having to fight the man who is claiming the land in a trial by battle. The grand assize means that twelve knights, who are chosen from the neighbours of the two disputing men, will have to answer one important question: Which of these two men has the best right to this land? The man they name must have the land and that is the final end of the dispute. No one else can claim the land.

We know what Henry did at Clarendon in 1166 and North-ampton in 1176 because he sent out special orders which we still have. We have a few more of his special orders, too, but it is difficult to find out all the day-to-day business he did because his Chancery clerks were not yet keeping records of it all – at least, if they did, the rolls are now lost. But there was so much business, and the king moved so fast, that it was becoming impossible to remember all that was done. It was easy to make muddles – giving the same gift twice over, forgetting exactly what the king had promised, giving contradictory orders. Remember that there were no carbon copies of important letters and documents: if you wanted a record you had to copy out again what you had already written. This was a burden, but by the reign of Henry's son John it had become absolutely necessary to keep a roll on which all the king's letters and documents were recorded. We have these rolls for John's reign, so we know more about what he did as he travelled about.

But the business was often the same, so let us look for a moment at one of John's journeys (or *eyres*, as they were called).

He started out from Woodstock in January 1205 and rode north through Northampton, Peterborough, Nottingham, right up to York. Turning round, he then circled southwards through the west down to Worcester, and rode back to Wood-stock on 24 March. All the way he did business, big and small: he consulted with some of his chief barons who came riding to meet him on the way, he settled a quarrel of the Archbishop of York, he decided to send off a baron, John Marshal, to Ire-land, he gave the great northern honour of Richmond to the Earl of Chester, and in the west he gave a castle to the Welsh prince, Llewellyn. Besides these important matters, we find him making gifts to his chaplains, letting a knight off from paying an unjust tax, giving a voucher for expenses to a servant who had looked after some royal horses, excusing some debts and declaring a young baron to be of age. This was the way medieval kings settled a great deal of their business, taking decisions with the advice of any servants and barons who happened to be present at that particular stage of the journey. 19

English Possessions
in France 1154-1223

C-County D-Duchy S-Seigniory V-Viscounty

0   50   100   150   200 miles

So far we have pictured Henry (and later his son John) riding round England. But, of course, Henry also ruled large parts of France. He succeeded the Norman kings, and so was Duke of Normandy; his father was Geoffrey of Anjou, from whom he inherited the title of Count of Anjou; his wife Eleanor brought him the Duchy of Aquitaine. If you look at the map on p. 20 you will see what a large part of France Henry ruled. For many years at a time Henry had to be away from England across the Channel, governing and defending his French lands. He moved about so rapidly that the French king was astonished, exclaiming on one occasion: 'Now in Ireland, now in England, now in Normandy, he must fly rather than travel by horse or ship!' Henry had to move quickly, otherwise he would never have kept up with the affairs of all his different lands. Even so, he had to be out of England a great deal and needed, above all things, trusted servants to govern it in his absence.

4 The King's Expenses and Income

Today when we want to know if we can pay our way, we make a balance-sheet, totting up on the left-hand side our income and on the right our expenditure. Then we 'strike a balance', that is, subtract whichever is the smaller sum from the bigger, and we feel cheerful if the smaller sum is our expenses because then the final figure is a credit balance. King Henry's clerks did not know how to do a balance-sheet like this. If they had I think they would nearly always have found themselves with an adverse balance, that is, one in which expenses were larger than income. Balance-sheet or no balance-sheet, the increasing royal expenses were their perpetual worry.

We can make a list of headings under which Henry's chief expenditure came. First of all, there were the expenses of all that enormous household, both in food and lodging and in wages. The chief officials got wages which seem very small to us. For instance, the Master Butler and Master Stewards got between 2s and 4s a day and the Master Chamberlain about the same. But a labourer then could live on as little as 1d a day, so 4s would be a good wage, and remember that with this went board and lodging and also special allowances of cakes, wine and candle-ends. Below the chief people there were the hordes of lesser servants who did not get much in wages but ate and drank enormously. Can you imagine the food bill for one week for this household? To the cost of the household we must also add the salaries or rewards of one kind or another which the king gave to the chief officers of government: the Justiciar, Treasurer, Chancellor, and an increasing number of judges.

Secondly, in order to impress people with his grandeur, King

Henry had to spend a great deal on rich robes, furs, jewellery, gold and silver cups, platters and so on. He probably did not care much about these things, but he knew that he must 'make a splash', as we say, because in those days a king's greatness was partly reckoned by how much treasure he possessed. We find, for instance, in his accounts for the year 1176, that he spent about £300 on scarlet cloth and furs. In the previous year he had given 'the young queen' (wife of his son Henry) sable furs and scarlet, while his daughter Joan's wedding dress, when she set out to marry the king of Sicily, cost £114. 4s 5d.

Thirdly, again partly to impress people, Henry had to make generous presents to his servants, his priests, his soldiers, and also to foreign kings and lords, to the Pope and to other important foreigners. For example, in 1176 he gave a palfrey to a messenger from the pope and soon after sent a present of hunting hounds to the Emperor of Constantinople. It was good business for a king to be generous, especially at festival times, such as Christmas and Easter. So we find records of many gifts in money to his servants at the great feast days.

Fourthly, the king had castles, hunting-lodges and manor houses which had to be kept in repair and sometimes rebuilt. The sheriff of each county, with his servants, usually looked after the building jobs, but the king also used to send round a special officer, a clerk of the works, to see that he was not being cheated. It was especially important that his castles should be in good repair – you will easily think why strong castles were essential. Building a new castle from scratch was even more expensive. Henry spent over £1,400 on building Orford Castle in Suffolk and for three years running he spent over £1,000 on Dover Castle.

Most important of all, and probably the greatest worry, was the king's army. Henry did not keep a large standing army all the time, though of course he always had a bodyguard for himself. But he spent so much of his reign fighting in France that he seemed for ever to be recruiting soldiers. When he got them for wages he had to pay them 8d a day, but we shall see in a moment that he had other ways of getting an army too.

How did Henry pay for all this? His chief problem was too little cash. Today this is not usually the main problem: if there is too little money around, the Bank of England prints more notes, though this of course makes other problems for us. But Henry had no paper money. For paying out, the Treasury only had the coin it received from the royal mints or that it managed to collect from other people. The coins used were silver pennies. They were packed in barrels and slowly carted to

A silver penny of Henry II. Can you read his name on the left-hand side?

where the money was needed. Once it took four carts and nineteen horses travelling many days to get enough money to the King. Silver *bullion* was often rather scarce, so there could be an actual shortage of coin. (This led, by the way, to various tricks, such as clipping bits off coins to melt down and make others, or making false money with base metal mixed in.) Henry's real wealth was in land, not money, and so he paid many of the people who served him, not in salaries, but in gifts of land. He also used important positions in the Church to reward his servants. The office of an archbishop or bishop had many lands belonging to it. He rewarded one of his most brilliant servants, Thomas Becket, by making him Archbishop of Canterbury. Here, as you probably know, Henry made a great mistake. On the other hand, Richard of Ilchester, after Henry made him Bishop of Winchester, served the King faithfully.

So the king made the church pay for some of his government. Besides these ways of paying, the king often had important people to give away. These were wards – young people under twenty-one who owned lands – and heiresses – rich girls and women who would bring their future husbands much wealth. To give away a wardship meant giving the right to enjoy all the profits of the ward's lands until he or she came of age. To give away an heiress meant, of course, marrying her to someone who then got all she owned. Wards and heiresses were not asked what they would like – they were just handed around like parcels. But they were often valuable parcels and Henry's servants liked getting them.

Charter of Henry II giving land

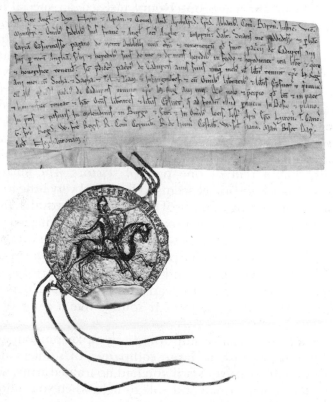

Henry also paid many lesser servants in land. He gave them a manor or a farm and instead of rent they had to do some special service for him. This was called holding land by *sergeaunty*. Sergeaunts did all sorts of services. Henry gave one servant, Boscher, the manor of Bericote in Warwickshire in return for rearing a white hound with red ears. At the end of the year he had to take it to the King, receiving instead another puppy to rear. The king's larderer at York did a number of jobs for his sergeaunty: he bought supplies when the king came to York, was a jailer for the prisoners, and also acted as a kind of bandmaster of all the *minstrels*. (He actually did so much that the king had to pay him 5*d* a day, besides his land.) A number of tenants had the duty of keeping falcons for the king. This sounds cheap and easy, but Henry insisted on special food for the birds: doves, pork and chicken, or even hares. In the Forest of Wychwood Alan Rasur was a royal forester holding land in return for the services of preparing for the royal hunts, collecting firewood and timber and catching trespassers. Nearby, a royal cook held the manor of Bletchingdon in return for providing the king with a dinner of roast pork whenever he hunted there. The king's tailor was paid with an estate in South Newington. Later, when another tailor held the same land, he had to make robes for the king and queen, mend the crown, and also pay a rent of one pair of scissors. The tenant of Kingston Russell in Dorset seems to have had very little to do – only to count the king's family of chessmen in the royal chamber and put them back into the box when Henry had finished playing on Christmas Day. But he was probably a servant with other duties as well. The king's harper was paid in land worth £13 a year. The king even gave land sometimes in return for tomfoolery: one tenant had to leap and whistle and dance on Christmas Day for his service. It sounds like a game of forfeits.

Land was also a most important way of keeping an army. To feed and pay cash to large companies of soldiers all the time was very expensive. Yet if you had no trained army, where could you get men armed and able to fight when you suddenly

Cavalry charge

needed to go to war? Much fighting in the twelfth century was on horseback and for this a knight had to keep expensive armour and weapons and be expert in managing his horse against the foe. Untrained men who fell off their horses at the first push, or mobs of peasants armed with pitchforks and knives were not much use in war. Henry's ancestors, William I and his sons, had partly solved this problem by giving land in return for military service. When the king summoned him, every baron was due to come to the assembly point complete with the number of knights he owed to the king, whether it was ten, twenty, thirty or more. These knights should be well armed and well trained in fighting. The usual rule was that they must be prepared to fight for forty days.

C

This scheme never worked very well. Kings always found they needed more soldiers than they could get this way and barons usually found that some of their knight-tenants did not want to fight: they might be too old or too young, or ill, or women, or churchmen, or just not keen on fighting. In order to make up the numbers properly Henry had to employ some paid soldiers (*mercenaries*) and he found it best to let off some barons and knights from doing their actual service. Instead, they had to pay a sum of money called *scutage* (it means shield-money from the Latin word 'scutum', a shield). With the scutage money Henry tried to pay his mercenaries, but he was nearly always short.

King Henry, you can see, needed money as well as land. How did he get it? In the first place, there were many small rents belonging to the king in places scattered all over the country. They were rents for markets and fairs, mills, firewood; some were paid instead of giving eggs or lambs or fish as in old days; most were only worth a few pence each. They hardly seemed worth collecting separately, so most of them had been lumped together in one sum, called a *farm*, which the sheriff of each county paid over to the royal treasury once a year. The sheriff might squeeze extra out of people, but the king only got the same sum year after year. This became less and less in value, since prices were rising and money therefore bought less (the same thing has been happening to our money over the last few years). Henry certainly could not meet his rising expenses on that old fixed income.

Luckily there were other ways of getting money and Henry (or perhaps his servants) was clever in thinking of new ones. One which went back to his Norman ancestors was taking a *relief*. When a baron died, his heir had to pay this sum called a relief to the king for the right to have his father's lands. The barons tried hard to get this sum fixed, but the kings in the past had been clever enough to stop their game. Henry I had promised his barons only to take a 'reasonable relief' but kept himself the right to decide what 'reasonable' meant. Naturally Henry II demanded as much as he could in reliefs, but he was too shrewd to ask for really outrageous sums, as his son John did later.

The king also had the right to ask for special taxes. There were three particular occasions when he could ask his barons for an aid to help him with extra expenses: when he knighted his eldest son, married his eldest daughter, or had to pay a ransom to free himself from an enemy's prison. Henry never had to claim the last, but his son Richard did. He could ask his barons for an aid on other occasions, too, and he could also squeeze special gifts out of the Church and from some of the Jews, as well as taxing his own manors and towns. He also had the right to put a tax on all the land in the country, but attempts at general taxation never brought in enough money. There were two reasons: first sheriffs and other collectors were apt to be dishonest; secondly, they did not have enough information about people's property to decide fairly what they ought to pay – to assess them properly, as we say. There were no income-tax returns in those days, and as far as the land tax was concerned, Henry's collectors only had the old Domesday Book assessment which was nearly a hundred years out of date. Henry did try to get some fresh information from landholders: his Chancery clerks sent to each baron a kind of questionnaire which they answered. When the answers had come in Henry tried to make some barons, at least, pay scutage on a higher assessment. Later, in the reigns of his two sons, Richard and John, royal officials began to improve the taxation by appointing good knights in every county to assess their neighbours and collect the taxes. Can you see the advantages of this system? Henry was sharp enough to see that people were now putting this wealth into moveable property – goods of all kinds – as well as land. So, right at the end of his reign, he brought in a new tax on these kinds of riches. It was called the Saladin tithe and was collected for the special purpose of sending a crusading army to fight the great Saracen warrior, Saladin, who had captured Jerusalem. Later kings copied this idea and used it to collect money for their own wars.

Lastly, Henry got quite a lot of money out of his law courts. 29

Dover Castle on which Henry II spent much money (see p. 23)

When the twelve men in each hundred accused thieves, robbers and murderers, the possessions (*chattels*) of the accused men became the king's property and were sold. When a landowner came to the chancery to ask for a writ of novel disseisin, he had to pay for it. If people did not turn up at court on the day for which they were summoned, they were fined. In many other ways, too, the king made money out of his courts. Henry was probably keen to improve the courts and give good justice, not only to make the country more peaceful, but also to make more money.

5 The Exchequer

We have seen that Henry's money came in from all sorts of places, in big sums and little sums, in good money often but sometimes in bad. One of Henry's worries was whether he was being robbed. He liked to know to the last farthing that his collectors had paid in everything. So he wanted very exact accounts kept. There were several reasons why this was difficult. One was the actual arithmetic. We use arabic numerals today, with a nought. Have you ever realised how much easier this makes addition and subtraction? Just try doing a big addition sum with Roman numerals, where there is no nought. For example, add up the following sum:

£	s	d
XXXIII	XII	VI
XLVI	V	XI
CLIX	XIX	VIII
CXCIV	VII	IX

The problem of keeping accounts had already been partly solved for Henry when he came to the throne. His grandfather, Henry I, had had a very clever servant, Roger le Poer or Roger of Salisbury, who started organising the king's accounting office. He was rewarded by being made bishop of Salisbury. Roger taught his skills to his nephew Nigel, Bishop of Ely, who in his turn passed them on to his son Richard FitzNigel (or Neal). So running the king's finances had become quite a family affair by the time Richard was made the royal Treasurer about 1158. He was Treasurer for nearly forty years and got to know the whole business from A to Z. You might not think that the king's accounts would be an exciting subject for a book, but the English way of doing it was the most up-to-date in Europe then and Richard was proud of it. So he decided to write a description of exactly how the king's money was managed.

Perhaps he really was asked by some curious young man to tell him the secrets, for this is how he begins his book:

> In the twenty-third year of the reign of King Henry II, as I was sitting at a turret window overlooking the Thames, someone said to me: Master! Why do you not teach others that knowledge of the *Exchequer* for which you are famous and put it in writing, lest it die with you?

After a bit of persuading Richard agreed and told the questioner (called the scholar) to sit down opposite him and ask questions. So the book is called the dialogue – the Dialogue of the Exchequer – and the very first question the scholar asks is: What is the Exchequer?

The Exchequer, says Richard, is really an oblong board, rather like a chess-board. It measures ten feet by five and has a rim about four finger-breadths in height to prevent anything falling off. Those who do the accounts use it as a table to sit round. On it is spread a special black cloth ruled with lines across and down, so forming a pattern of checks. This cloth is the real exchequer, but now the name is given to the whole office in which the king's accounts are done. It is, as we should say, the king's financial department.

As you will see a little later, the checked cloth makes the arithmetic much easier. It was probably brought in by Richard's grandfather, Roger. The name exchequer comes, of course, from the checked or chess-board pattern. The Scholar asks Richard: Why not name it after a draughts board? Well, says Richard, the whole business really is like a game of chess. Facing each other across the board are the Treasurer and the sheriff. They play a game against each other: the Treasurer wants to get as much money as possible out of the sheriff and the sheriff wants to pay as little as possible. The chess-men are counters which stand for sums of money and as

Chess pieces

these are moved up and down the rest of the committee sit round the board to see that the rules of the game are kept.

The sheriff is the chief collector of the king's money in each county and so it is chiefly against sheriffs that the Treasurer plays the king's game of detecting fraud and squeezing out the full sum due, though other people are also summoned to the 33

Exchequer. England in Henry's reign is already divided into counties (or shires). The sheriff is the king's head official in each county. He has many things to do, but one of the most important is to collect all the king's different moneys or revenues. Some of these he collects by a method called farming, that is, he pays a lump sum to the Exchequer and collects as much as he can. Can you see why, on the whole, the sheriff likes this system and the Treasurer does not? But there are many other separate sums he has to pay in as well. There are profits from the royal lands and perhaps from those of some wards and heiresses in the king's care. If criminals have been caught and punished, the sheriff has to sell their goods and pay in the amount. There may be treasure-trove which belongs to the king or – on the sea-shore – an extra large fish which also has to be claimed for the king. There may be some special tax to collect, a scutage or an aid. Altogether there will be many items and the treasurer will nose them all out to make sure the king loses nothing.

There is another complication: the sheriff will also have spent money for the king – on his castles, his manors or other matters. When he appears to play the Exchequer game, the sheriff has to deduct what he has paid out from money he has received. Of course he always wants to make the deductions as big as possible. If he can end up with the king owing him money, this is splendid. But equally the Treasurer, playing against him aims at reducing the deductions so as to end up with the sheriff paying the king. The game ends when both sides agree on the final figure.

HOW THE EXCHEQUER WORKS

First, the people who have to come must be summoned. On one side, there are the king's officials, barons of the Exchequer, who have to sit and judge. On the other side there are the sheriffs who come to be judged and to pay. The summons is a writ or letter in Latin on a strip of parchment with the royal seal hanging from it. The sheriff's summons reads like this: 'Henry King of England to such-and-such sheriff greeting. See that, as you love yourself and all that you have, you be at the Exchequer on the morrow of Michaelmas and have with you whatever you owe.'

Michaelmas is the most important meeting when the sheriff really has to account for all the year's money. You can find out from a calendar which day in September this is. In order to watch the sheriffs closely enough, there is also a half-yearly meeting on the Monday after Low Sunday, which is the next Sunday to Easter.

So now imagine the sheriff of Norfolk, or Wiltshire, or some other county, riding up to Westminster with his bags bumping beside the saddle. They are very important bags, containing money, accounts and things called *tallies* which you will soon read about. He is anxious not to meet robbers on the road; he is also anxious to arrive punctually. He must appear before the barons on exactly the right day, otherwise he will have to pay 100s for one day missed, and worse if he is later.

He turns up at the Exchequer with all his bags and first of all he must go to the Lower Exchequer. Here the Treasurer's Clerk takes his money bags and has the money tipped out in a heap. The coins are counted by four tellers, weighed in wooden bowls and finally sealed up in parchment packets holding £100 each. But before that, the pile of coins is well mixed up and a sample of the silver taken out in order to test that it is all good metal. This test is called the *assay*. An official called the Knight-Silversmith weighs the sample of £1 and then takes it

Weighing money at the Exchequer

to the Melter. The sheriff goes with him and two other sheriffs as well to see that the test is fairly done. The Melter has to melt down the silver coins over a fire to just the right point, while the sheriff watches sharply to see that he does not over-heat and so waste the silver. When the coins have been melted into one bar of silver, this is weighed again. If it weighs less than it did as coins, then the sheriff must pay the difference on every £1 of coins.

You will be wondering why so much trouble is taken over the actual coins. Today, when we pay money into a bank, the clerk as a rule only counts it. But in the days of King Henry there was a good deal of bad money about, both false money made out of cheaper metal, and money which was short in weight because bits had been clipped off it. The men in the Lower Exchequer were there to see that every £100 paid in by the sheriffs had the right amount of silver, the right weight and the right number of coins.

The treasurer's clerk watches all these proceedings very sharply and when he is satisfied he records in writing exactly how much has been received. Then he tells the tally-cutter to make a tally for this amount. A tally is a kind of receipt on a piece of wood. It looks like this:

The sum of money is recorded on it by notches cut across the stick. For £1000 the piece cut away must be wide enough to hold the thickness of the palm of a hand. For £100 it must be the thickness of a thumb, for £20 the thickness of a little finger, for £1 that of a swelling barleycorn. A shilling is shown by a small notch and a penny by a single cut. When the tally has been cut it is split downwards, across the notches into two

36 pieces, the foil and the stock. The sheriff is given the foil and

the Treasury keeps the stock. If there is any dispute later the two halves of the tally must be produced and put together. They ought to match exactly, and if one side has been trying to alter the notches this should show at once.

When the money has finally been sealed up in packets and recorded, the knights of the Lower Exchequer lock it up in one of the chests. Each chest has two different locks with two different keys, one held by each knight. No chest can be opened without both of them. What is more, each chest also has a strap round it which is sealed with the treasurer's seal after locking the chest. So when it is opened three people have to be present: the treasurer's clerk to break the seal and the two knights with their keys. You will quickly see why there is all this elaborate arrangement.

With the money safely stored, the sheriff goes to the Upper Exchequer for the really serious part of the business. When he enters the room only his clerk is allowed in with him and then the door is firmly shut by the usher. The sheriff sees in front of him the exchequer-board table with four benches round the four sides. On three sides sit the barons of the Exchequer and their officials. They have sharp, hard faces and the sheriff may well feel nervous, especially if he has something to hide. He sits down in the middle of the bench at the end of the board and straight opposite him at the top end is the chief justiciar, the most important man in the kingdom after the king, and the president of the Exchequer. On his left the bench sticks out beyond the table and on it sits the chancellor, the constable, two chamberlains and the marshal. On his right is the Bishop of Winchester. He sits there for a special purpose. Next to him, round the corner on the long side of the table, is the treasurer. The bishop's job is to watch him carefully to see that he does his duty, for sometimes he might try to cheat, or again he is often so hard-working that he might fall asleep. The treasurer is, you remember, the chief player against the sheriff. It is most important that his record or roll, on which all the accounts are entered, should be accurate. So his scribe sits next to him to write his roll. In order to have a check, another

In the Black Book of the Exchequer the writer drew St John looking exactly like an Exchequer scribe (except for his wings)

roll is kept, called the Chancery Roll, so the scribe of the Chancery Roll sits next to the treasurer's scribe, and next to him again is the chancellor's clerk who watches sharply to see that the two rolls are exactly the same, even in dotting the 'i's and crossing the 't's. Even this amount of checking does not satisfy the king and now there is a third roll kept by Master Thomas Brown who sits beside the sheriff, on the bench to his left. There is no room for Thomas Brown's scribe who writes the roll, so he has to sit up behind and peer over the Treasurer's scribe's shoulder with sharp eyes, to copy down the account from him.

On the sheriff's right is his own clerk to see that he is not cheated and then down the other long side of the table are other clerks and servants with special duties. One is the cutter of tallies, another the calculator with his counters, ready to do the sums on the board and at the end nearest the sheriff sits the master of the Writing Office. Now here is a diagram to show where everyone sits. Study it and try to picture all those men sitting on their benches round the board.

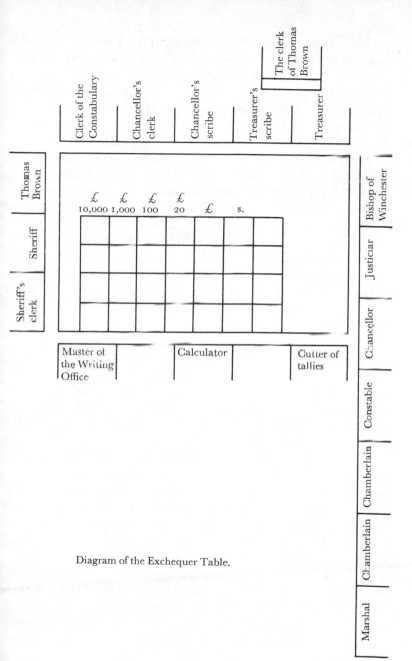

Diagram of the Exchequer Table.

The treasurer makes the first move in the game by asking the sheriff if he is ready to render his account. The sheriff answers: 'I am ready.' The treasurer then asks about fixed payments and grants of land. These are sums of money and lands which the sheriff, by the king's command, has given to various people in his county. Some will be wages paid to servants, for instance, to a keeper of a royal palace, to royal pipers, or to a servant called a wolf-taker. Other grants will be alms given to poor people. If these grants are the same as last year, the treasurer's scribe will copy them into the new account, closely watched by all those checking him. If the sheriff has made new grants, he must produce a writ from the king ordering him to do so. Each writ is read aloud by the treasurer's clerk before it is copied into the roll. Next, the treasurer asks the sheriff what other expenses he has had. The sheriff has probably paid out money to deal with criminals, perhaps for carts to take them from one place to another. Or again, a sheriff in a coastal county may have had to transport a large royal fish and buy salt for salting it. Or he may have been ordered to repair a castle. In this case the wily barons of the Exchequer will not be satisfied until they have summoned the man who actually saw the work done (called the keeper of the works) and made him swear that the money has been paid out. Thus the treasurer and the sheriff go through all the money spent by the sheriff and it is entered in the roll.

Then the treasurer starts on what the sheriff owes to the Exchequer. First, he goes back to last year's account and if there is still something owing makes the sheriff agree to pay this. Then he begins asking about this year's income. Have any landowners been encroaching on the king's property? If so, how much did the sheriff fine them? Are there any *escheats* and if so, how much income did the sheriff take from these lands? Are there any lands which are in the king's wardship and if so, what income has the sheriff collected from these? (In this case the sheriff is allowed to keep enough of the income to house and feed the heir, but he must hand over the rest.) If an heir has come of age during the last year, he should have paid a sum called a relief for the right to take his own lands. Of course the treasurer asks the sheriff if he has any reliefs to pay in. Then he asks about the value of chattels belonging to any criminals that may have been caught, for the sheriff must pay in the sum he sold them for as well. The sheriff must also account for all the fines he has taken from people brought before the courts of justice and all the debts he has collected from men who owe money to the king. Often he has not been able to get the full amount from them and then the item has to be carried over in the account till next year. So the questioning goes on and for each item the sheriff has to say how much he has taken and produce tallies as receipts to prove what he says. Sometimes he argues about a sum, declaring that he has not received as much as the Treasurer says; sometimes the Treasurer accuses him of giving too low a figure.

So far all these are special sums of money, that is, they do not turn up regularly each year. There is also the regular income from royal manors, forests, towns, markets and so on. Many of these, as you know, are lumped together as the farm. Probably in accounting for the special payments the sheriff often gets the worst of the deal, for the Treasurer and the other barons are on the alert to nose out sums the sheriff is trying to conceal. But when it comes to the farm, the sheriff gets the best of the game, for the farm has been fixed by a bargain and it is very difficult to increase the lump sum the sheriff has to pay, even though the treasurer may know perfectly well that the sheriff is able to make a handsome profit on what he actually collects from people.

All this time, while the argument between the treasurer and the sheriff has been going on, the calculator has been sitting with piles of little counters in front of him, placing them in the columns of the checked board and moving them up and down as the different sums of money are agreed. Everyone can see what he is doing. In the right-hand column he puts the pence, counting up to eleven, in the next the shillings and the third the pounds. The pounds column is straight in front of him, for he uses it most often. Then further to the left, the fourth column is for scores of pounds, the fifth for hundreds, the sixth for thousands and the seventh (not often used) for tens of thousands of pounds. He counts aloud as he moves the counter up the columns, or, as he reaches the top of one column, moves the counter to the bottom of the next one. Everyone watches sharply, for a little push could alter shillings into pounds and so on.

At the same time, sitting on the opposite side, the Treasurer's scribe has been writing the account, as dictated by the treasurer. This account is kept on pieces of sheepskin joined at the top. This is called a pipe roll because when rolled up, it looks rather like a drain-pipe. Each roll is about 13 inches wide. The scribe has to be very careful and if by chance he makes

A Pipe Roll

Part of a Pipe Roll. Can you discover to which countie this belongs and where it says (in Latin) 'And he is quit'?

a mistake, he dare not scratch it out, but must cancel it with a fine line and put in the correction. Indeed, sheepskin is purposely used for the pipe rolls because if anyone tries to make an *erasure* it shows plainly. On the pipe roll each account is headed by the name of the county, then the name of the sheriff. Then follow, first all the sheriff's payments, and then the amount of this year's farm. Then, if there is any old farm to pay, this is added. After a space of six lines, the list of all the special income received by the sheriff follows. Finally, the solemn moment of finishing the account arrives. All the sums the sheriff has paid are added up and deducted from all the sums he is due to pay, leaving one total sum which he owes. Then the value of the actual cash he has brought and which, you remember, has already been counted, weighed and assayed, is agreed upon. And so the conclusion of the business is reached. If the money paid in by the sheriff balances what he owes, the clerk writes in a large hand at the end of the account AND HE IS QUIT. If the sheriff still owes something, he writes: AND HE OWES. . . . Last of all, the amount the sheriff has paid into the Treasury is added and the sheriff takes an oath to abide by the account. The game is over, the sheriff is dismissed and rides off home, glad to be through with it until next Easter.

6 The Sheriff in the County

When the sheriff rode back to his county he had plenty to do.
England had for centuries been divided into shires, or counties,
as the Normans called them. The sheriff, first called shire-reeve,
had now become the chief official in each county to carry out
the king's government. He had a staff of under-officers to help
him. A very important part of his work, as we have seen, was
to collect the king's income and pay his expenses in the county.
Other regular jobs he had to do were to see that the king's
castles were in good repair, guarded and supplied with food;
to keep prisoners in his gaol until they could be tried; to look
after the property of the king's wards in his county; to see
that good coins were being used and not bad.

The sheriff had some particularly important duties to do
with justice. Each county was divided into districts called
hundreds and in each hundred the sheriff held a court (unless
the king had given the hundred to a baron). One of the main
purposes of this was to keep peace in the county. Since there
was no paid police force, all the people had to help with police
work. If the cry of 'Thief! Thief!' was raised, each person had
to drop what he was doing in order to chase the thief. This was
known as the hue and cry. But many wrong-doers were neither
seen nor caught. There was another way of catching criminals.
In each village men and boys over the age of fifteen were put
in groups of about ten, called *tithings*, with a head man to each
group. Each member swore to report anything wrong done by
any other member. When the sheriff held his court, called the
tourn, all the head men of the tithings, as well as four
villagers and the *reeve* to represent each village, had to come to

the court and make their reports. If they reported that one of their members had committed a crime, they had to bring him along to make sure that he did not run away. If they reported little faults, petty crimes, like trespassing or hitting someone on the nose, then the sheriff quickly judged and punished the wrong-doer. After Henry sent out his orders from Clarendon in 1166, the court of the hundred had another task given to it. The members had to report serious crimes, such as murder, robbery or thieving, and these were generally kept to be tried by the king's justice when he came round. So the people of the hundred court had to choose twelve trustworthy men from among themselves to make a solemn accusation against the suspected people in the presence of the king's justice. It was a serious duty, for if they made a mistake the accusers might be punished themselves. But the royal command insisted that these twelve men, the *jury of accusation*, should give the opinion of their hundred in this way.

The sheriff held a county court too, but less often than the hundred court. He summoned to this court all the free land-holders in the county, the twelve from each hundred and *representatives* from each village and town. One of the reasons for holding a county court was to hear the royal commands. King Henry found it especially useful to send his orders to the county court so that everyone would know them. Remember that with no radio, newspapers, telegraph or speedy post, one of the king's great problems was letting people know what he had decided. So he ordered his chancery clerks to send out his commands in letters or writs to each sheriff. They wrote firmly on a piece of parchment in crisp, clear Latin – the kind of letter that demanded instant obedience. The chancellor sealed it with the King's Seal and soon a royal messenger was thundering along the road on his quickest horse. If it was a command to one particular sheriff about a special matter, he might not need to call the county court at all. He would have to do what the writ said – *execute the writ* we say – as soon as possible. It might be to make a delaying baron pay up

the scutage he owed in double quick time or to send a cartload

A King's Messenger delivering a writ

of wine to one of the royal hunting lodges. But if the king wanted to send out a general command to all, then the chancery clerks would have many writs to write and many king's messengers would go galloping out of the palace gates, riding in all directions to take copies of the writ to all the sheriffs. The king's orders would be read at the county court. Probably the orders made at Clarendon and Northampton were sent out in this way.

In 1181 Henry made another set of commands which must have gone to the counties in this way. This was called the Assize of Arms. Henry collected the armies he wanted for wars in France from his barons and from paid mercenaries. But it was a very ancient custom in England that all free men should have weapons and be ready to fight for their homes if an enemy invaded the country or powerful men rebelled. One of the sheriff's jobs was to drill these people and see that they had good weapons. Perhaps Henry heard that the sheriffs were getting slack about this. You can imagine that peaceful farmers, busy with their crops, did not want to drill or spend time putting their spears and knives in cutting order. On the other

hand, if the Welsh invaded Herefordshire, for instance, it was no good meeting them with men who did not know how to fight or only had broken weapons. Henry decided to put the county *militia* into good fighting trim. His Assize of Arms commanded that before a certain date all the freemen were to swear that they had the right weapons and that they would fight loyally for the king. The Assize said exactly what kind of arms each man had to possess, according to his wealth and class. Thus a knight, or a man with the same amount of land, had to have a *hauberk*, a helmet, a shield and a lance; a man who had possessions worth 10 *marks* must have an *aubergel*, a *head piece of iron* and a lance; townsmen and the rest of the freemen must have a *quilted doublet*, a headpiece of iron and a lance. In each place a kind of jury of neighbours was called to decide in which group everyone should be put. Then they were all enrolled on a long list and swore

Knight in armour, showing hauberk, helmet and shield

their oaths to keep the king's Assize. Do you think this was a good plan? Can you see any dangers in it?

Henry's sheriffs had to be tough men. Sometimes the king used important people, earls and barons, as his sheriffs. More often they were royal servants who had learnt the king's business in the Chancery or Treasury. Can you see why Henry liked this kind of man as sheriff? These sheriffs were often hard, sharp men, quick to spot anyone trying to cheat them, ready to drive hard bargains. It was tempting to try and make as much money as possible for yourself and so the sheriffs themselves often cheated the king. As you know, the Exchequer officials had ways of finding out the sheriffs who did not pay over to the royal Treasury all they should. But King Henry suspected that too many were getting away with dishonesty. So in 1170 he held a grand enquiry, called the *Inquest* of Sheriffs. His Justices went all round the country with a long list of questions which they put to all the barons, knights and freemen in each county. They asked questions like these: how much land has the sheriff bought; who has been collecting taxes; has the sheriff been taking bribes? All the county people had to swear to tell the truth. Do you think this was a good way to get at the truth? Evidently Henry found out a great deal, for he sacked many sheriffs and put new ones in their place. It was a very difficult problem, for even some of his most faithful men were often tempted to make a profit for themselves. In 1178 one of Henry's best servants, Ranulf Glanville, who had been a sheriff as well as the royal Justiciar, was accused of pocketing £1,571 1s 1d, as well as taking silver plate, horses and hawks which ought to have gone to the king! Perhaps we should not be too severe with the dishonest ones: they had to work very hard, they often lost money instead of making it and the king could not have governed the country without them.

7 The King's Justice

When we speak of the king or his officers or the barons 'doing justice' we mean that they acted as judges to settle many different kinds of problem. It might be a case of two men disputing over a piece of land, or of someone complaining that he has been wronged in some way: judging such disputes between people is called *civil justice*. But if a man was accused of murder or theft, or of wronging the king in some way, these cases usually came under the heading of *criminal justice*. Some civil and some criminal cases (usually the less serious ones) could be tried by sheriffs, barons and others in the smaller courts all over the country. But important disputes, serious crimes and wrongs done to the king were kept for the king himself to judge or his officers. He had a special team of officers called justices, with a chief, called the justiciar, over them.

Wherever the king was he could hold a court to do justice. Sometimes people with complaints had to follow him round from place to place for years before Henry had time to hear their case. One man, Richard of Anesti, tried for five years to get his claim to some lands settled. He has left us the whole story of his journeyings written on parchment. The dispute was about property which his uncle had left him in his will but which was being held by his uncle's daughter. Richard was pushed around from pillar to post trying to prove his right to the land. Altogether on his own travelling, on the messengers he sent and on presents to people who might help him, he spent more than £200 (a lot of money in those days). Finally, one day when the king was doing justice at Woodstock, Richard of Anesti got his case heard and the court judged that he should have his uncle's land. The only trouble was that he had probably spent and borrowed from Jews more money than the land was worth.

Imagine now that you are attending the king's court which, on this occasion, is being held in the Great Hall at Westminster. The lower part of the hall is crowded with barons, courtiers, churchmen and citizens of London sitting on benches. At the top end there is a high throne richly decorated for the king and on either side of it benches covered with red and gold cloth on which the king's chief councillors sit. The Archbishop of Canterbury is there and Richard de Luci, the justiciar, the chancellor, the treasurer and others. At a table sit the writing-clerks with parchment, quills and inkhorns to keep a record. Today the king will judge a very serious case. Two or three nights ago some Londoners broke into the house of a baron, Robert de Stuteville. But he, hearing the noise they were making smashing in the door, was ready for them, all armed with his servants, when they finally got in. He caught one of them, while the rest ran away. But the captured thief turned informer and gave the names of the others, so that five of them were arrested and on this day have been brought for trial. The king is very angry for he hates above all things people who break his peace and act violently. Now the prisoners are brought into court. The informer appeals them (that is, accuses them) of the crime. They deny it but are sent to the ordeal by boiling water. Two in terror refuse the ordeal and are at once judged guilty and hurried off to execution by hanging. The other three manage the ordeal and so are kept prisoners for three days to see if they have succeeded in 'proving' their innocence.

Much of the king's justice was done by his officers, either sitting in Westminster or going round the country to the local courts. When Henry was in England, he paid particular attention to the way his officers were behaving and how his justices were doing justice. We have already heard how he held an Inquest of sheriffs. He also held courts in which he asked sharp questions about justice: were his justices doing good justice; were people getting their complaints settled; were the justices coming round too often or too seldom? When people complained, he changed the arrangements. For instance, one plan had been to divide England into six parts (called *circuits*), with three justices going round each. But a later plan was to have four circuits, with five or six justices to each. One great problem was that people tried to bribe the justices, so the king had to try and find men who would not take bribes. Sometimes he used bishops and abbots, sometimes earls and barons, sometimes his own court servants. A man who watched Henry closely, Ralph de Diceto, dean of St Paul's, said that he wanted justices who would turn neither to the right hand nor to the left, not oppressing the poor in their judgments, nor favouring the rich by taking bribes. Sometimes he got these *incorruptible* justices; sometimes he did not. But when they came round through the shires they did strike terror into the hearts of wrong-doers, as Ralph tells us, and punish those who had cheated the king.

The justices on eyre (that is, travelling round) had to work hard. Here is an account of some of the business done by Richard de Luci and Geoffrey de Mandeville, Earl of Essex, going round the eastern and northern counties in 1166. First of all, in each county they had to find out if the sheriffs had been catching and holding for trial all suspected thieves, robbers, murderers and other criminals. It was often difficult to get at the truth. When a sheriff reported only three well-off men who were accused of serious crimes, the justices suspected that he had been bribed to let off the other rich ones. Another problem was that so many of the accused had been allowed to get away. In Lincolnshire, for instance, nearly all the accused had run away. This was a great headache for the justices, since they then had to collect fines from all those who had been *sureties* for the runaways. Also in Lincolnshire they collected fines from a group of people who had made a scuffle and a great row, from a man who ran away from a trial by battle, and from people who had concealed murderers. When they reached Yorkshire they found a great mix-up of business to be done: a man had kept a whale washed up on the shore, instead of handing it over as the property of the king; at Malsonby some villagers had actually ploughed up the king's highway; elsewhere a man had been trying to pass off a bad penny. All these had to be punished, as well as the men of Harthill who hid a runaway from justice. A young landowner came to pay five marks for the land he had inherited from his father; another man pretended he had not been summoned to the court when he had; somebody else had been poaching on royal marshland and had been caught. Besides trying serious crimes, you see, the king's justices had to have their eyes on all sorts of matters which concerned the king. We know about all these things because the money collected by the justices had to come back to the exchequer, where all the different fines were carefully entered on the pipe roll.

Travelling round the country the king and his justices must have seen many men whose clothes showed that they were churchmen – bishops, abbots, monks, priests, deacons. There were a great many of them in England. They made a special problem for King Henry because they owed obedience to the Pope, the head of the Church, as well as to the king. Henry himself had a duty to obey the Church. Do you remember that at his coronation he put himself under God and the Law? This meant that the Archbishop of Canterbury, the head of the church in England, and the Pope, the head of the whole Church, had the right to tell Henry what he ought to do and what he ought not to do. But suppose churchmen in England broke the king's law and the Archbishop forebade the king to punish them, what could Henry do? This was just what happened. At the time when King Henry was trying hard to stop crime and bring all criminals to justice, some churchmen were escaping from his punishment by claiming that they could only be tried in a church court. If a churchman committed a murder or theft, the church court which tried him would not be able to pronounce the death penalty or give him a severe sentence. The worst punishment he could get was to have his rank as a churchman taken away, so that he could no longer be protected if he committed another crime.

The king's justices reported to Henry cases where criminals were not being properly punished because they were churchmen, or clerks, as they were called. There was, for instance, the case of a canon of Bedford, named Philip of Brois, who was tried in a Church court for the murder of a knight of Dunstable. He got off, as not guilty, but then was brought to the king's court for a second trial. There he insulted the royal justice and when the king complained, the Archbishop of Canterbury protected him. This archbishop was Thomas Becket about whom you will be reading in a little while. The question of punishing clerks who committed crimes was not the only point on which Henry found the Church opposing him. The Pope held the highest Church court and men had begun to take certain kinds of dispute to the Pope's court for settlement. This was called 'appealing to Rome'. Henry, of course, wished to be master in his own kingdom and therefore opposed any appeal going to Rome without his permission.

King Henry did not want to quarrel with the Church. The Pope and the bishops could help him in governing the country. But, although God's law was higher, Henry intended his own will to be law in England. So he looked for ways to make the Church do what he wanted. He thought he had found the right way when he made Thomas Becket, his friend, Archbishop of Canterbury. But the new Archbishop began opposing Henry's will at once. Then the king thought he would put down in writing all the points on which he wanted the Archbishop and the Pope to agree to his rights. He was careful not to ask for too much. For instance, over clerks committing crimes, he did not ask to try them in his own court, but only to be able to punish them properly if they were found guilty. He presented all his points to Becket in a writing called the Constitutions of Clarendon. But Becket and the Pope found some of the points against the law of the Church which they believed was the law of God. They would not give in.

The final battle took place in a great council at Northampton to which the king had summoned all his barons and bishops. Picture King Henry, seated with scowling face, in his

This picture shows Becket in France, arguing with King Henry and King Louis of France

royal chair, and his lords on rows of benches around him; over against him, the Archbishop is seated with all his clerks around him; finally, there are the rest of the bishops, worried and unhappy, hovering between the king and the Archbishop, because they were not sure which to obey. Now Henry was no longer moderate: he was angry and brought harsh accusations against his archbishop. The Council went on for several days. On the last day Becket entered the hall carrying his archbishop's cross as a sign that, if the king's power lay in his sword, the Archbishop's lay in the Cross of Christ. This made Henry even angrier. Finally, after bitter argument, Becket strode out of the Council. No one stopped him and he was able to get out of England in disguise. He crossed the Channel to France and appealed to the Pope.

The law of the Church and the law of the king seemed to have clashed absolutely. The rest of the story of Henry's quarrel with Thomas Becket is told on p. 71–2. When Becket was dead and the King had to make his peace with the Pope he was forced to admit some of the rights of Church law in his kingdom: clerks who committed crimes were to be tried and punished in Church courts, not royal ones; appeals were to go freely to Rome. But when tempers had cooled down and on both sides men could look at the problem without anger, they were able to

55

find ways in which the Church and the king could get on quite well together. The king's law and justice were not badly weakened by the Church law – indeed, in many ways the Church helped the king. But the great problem of whether a king or ruler owes obedience to any higher law (not necessarily the Pope's or the Archbishop's law but God's law) is still an important one.

8 The City of London in Henry II's Time

When Henry held his court at Westminster he was not inside
the City of London but nearly on its doorstep, about two miles
away. To go from London to Westminster you rode out of the
city gate on the west – Ludgate – along Fleet Street, through
the little village of Charing and then through orchards and
gardens to the palace of Westminster and the great Abbey
beside it. It was a good thing that Henry's palace was not inside
the city. London was the largest town in England and it was
growing. Other towns were growing too, for craftsmen were
making more things to sell and merchants were marketing
more food and wine, more wool and cloth, more goods of all
kinds made by the craftsmen. The king liked rich towns because
he could tax their riches, but he did not want disobedient towns
that rebelled against him. So he would not let many towns
manage their own affairs without his sheriffs coming in to see
what they were up to. Above all, he watched London very
sharply, taking care to live outside it but keeping his thumb
on the city tightly. For London had been very uppish in the
days when Henry's mother, Matilda, and King Stephen had
been fighting for the crown, and Henry was determined to keep
it down. Living outside, he could keep clear of city trouble but
he had a good hold on it through the Tower of London, that
great castle from which the king's soldiers could clatter out
at a moment's notice to stop rebellion. Under the king's eye
the London citizens managed most of their own affairs, provid-
ed they paid promptly the taxes which the king demanded
from them. But when they would not – or could not – stop
violent crimes, like that of the men who broke into Robert de 57

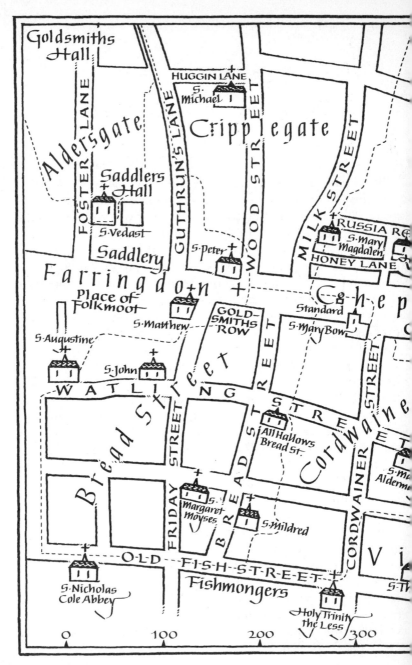

Plan of London streets, showing where different trades were found

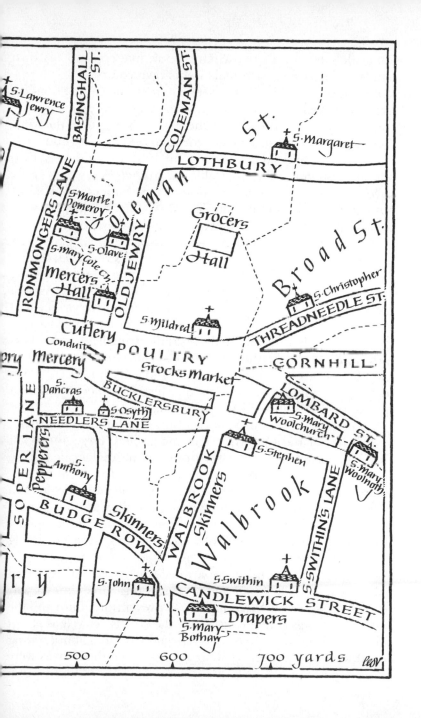

Stuteville's house, then the king took matters into his own hands and punished criminals in his own courts.

Except on the side of the river Thames, the City of London had a stout wall all round it, with seven gates by which people could enter. From Aldgate in the east to Newgate in the west, there was one main street right through the city, with hundreds of tiny streets and lanes running off it, down to the river on one side and out to the city wall on the other. You would easily have got lost in this maze. The houses were built of wood below but the top part was usually just a wooden framework with plaster filling in between. Roofs were thatched with straw or reeds, and windows just had wooden shutters, no glass. The pointed gables of the houses overhung the streets, darkening them greatly. In most of these houses the ground floor was the shop or workroom, while the family lived upstairs. Almost every man was a craftsman or a trader and in order to see that work was honestly done, all the people in one trade lived in one street or lane. For instance, all the saddlers and leather-workers were in St Martin's, the cappers in Fleet Street, the *fullers* in Candlewick Street and all the *vintners* and cookshops were down by the river. A man named Fitz-Stephen who knew London at this time tells us about a famous cookshop:

> There daily you may find food according to the season, dishes of meat, roast, fried and boiled, large and small fish, coarser meats for the poor and more delicate for the rich, such as venison, and big and small birds.

There were also several open markets for vegetables brought in from the country, for poultry and eggs, and at Billingsgate, by the river, for fish. Here everything sold had to be openly displayed so that buyers could see that they were not being cheated.

The citizens of London took much care over making good rules for trade. They had a general meeting three times a year to make laws about such matters as prevention of fire and the nuisance of pigs wandering about the streets, as well as about buying and selling. There were special city rules about selling bread and ale. Inspectors went round to see that loaves were

Baking

full weight and that ale had not been watered. Each craftsman was kept strictly to the one thing he was allowed to make, so the saddler, for instance, could not make shoes and the weaver must not dye the cloth he wove.

The workers in three trades – the bakers, the fishmongers and the weavers – had now formed themselves into *guilds*. They had their own meetings and made their own rules. They protected themselves by fixing prices but they also protected customers by punishing guildsmen who sold bad stuff. The king had given his consent to these three guilds and he made money out of them by making them buy a licence. Other trades, for instance the goldsmiths and the pepperers, were trying to make guilds on the sly without paying for them. King Henry's sheriffs in London, however, were quick to find out what was going on, and so we find written in the Pipe Roll of 1180 a long list of fines which the new guilds had to pay to the king.

A cloth shop

Selling furs

Generally, however, the king left the citizens to make their own rules, but the London merchants who wanted to trade outside the country must buy from the king a licence to export, and pay customs duties on the goods they sent overseas. The Thames was a beautiful wide river for ships. More and more ships were now sailing in and out of London port, bringing in furs, spices, rich silks, and wine, and taking out wool, cloth, corn, tin, fish, and cheese. If the ships that came in were foreign ones with foreign merchants, these men must pay for a special licence from the king. Some foreigners, Flemings from Flanders, settled in London as weavers and dyers of cloth. The Londoners did not like them, but the king made money out of them and so he was prepared to protect them.

A twelfth-century ship

When King Henry and his court were at Westminster there was plenty to see in London. Since they almost lived on horseback, perhaps the most interesting thing was the great horse-fair, held every week just outside the city gate in an open space called Smoothfield (Smithfield). Everyone, nobleman and citizen, trooped out to it. Fitz-Stephen thought it was a beautiful sight:

> It is pleasant to see the high-stepping palfreys with their gleaming coats, as they go through their paces, putting down their feet alternately on one side together. Next one can see the horses fit for esquires, moving faster though less smoothly, lifting up and setting down, as it were, the opposite fore and hind feet: here are colts of fine breed,

Restive horses

> but not yet accustomed to the bit, stepping high with jaunty tread; there are the *sumpter-horses*, powerful and spirited; and after them the war-horses, costly, elegant of form, noble of stature, with ears quickly *tremulous*, necks arched and large haunches. When a race is about to begin a shout is raised. The horses enter into the spirit of the contest. Their limbs tremble and so impatient are they of delay that they cannot keep still. When the signal is

given, they stretch their limbs to the uttermost and dash down the course with courageous speed.

By themselves in another part of the field stand the goods of the countryfolk: tools of *husbandry*, *swine* with long flanks, cows with full udders, oxen of immense size and woolly sheep. There also stand the mares fit for the plough, some big with foal and others with brisk young colts closely following them.

London, according to Fitz-Stephen, was a very sporting city. He tells us a lot about the different amusements at various times of the year. On Shrove Tuesday the schoolboys had a carnival day when they went to school with their own fighting cocks tucked under their arms. All the morning they watched cock-fights in school – this was better than learning long Latin speeches by heart! After dinner they all went out into the fields beyond the walls to play football, one school against another, and their elders came out to watch. On Sundays in Lent there were tournaments and mock battles in the fields. If the king's court was at Westminster swarms of gay young courtiers rode along the Strand on their war-horses to join the young men of the city and they all crowded out through Newgate with lances and shields to play at fighting. The noise was terrific, with horses neighing and pawing the ground, and boys shouting. First they had single fights in which two young men rode furiously at each other with their headless lances. After a time

Jousting

everyone joined in a general scrum in which different bands wheeled and circled round, charging and pursuing each other, while the trampling hooves rang and the sparks flew. The courtiers fought against the citizens, usually in a quite good-tempered way, but sometimes bad feeling flared up and someone was seriously hurt.

At Easter time the fun was on the river. A shield was fixed to a tree in mid-stream and the young men rowed swiftly towards it in small boats. One member of the crew stood up in the rocking boat and tried to strike the shield, as the boat shot by it, without falling in the river. This was very difficult to do and he usually took a header into the water. Two boats were

moored by the target, with people all ready to fish out those who fell in. On the bridge and banks the crowds of spectators laughed their heads off as the dripping lads were hauled aboard.

On feast days in the summer the young men sported in the fields outside the city – running,

Wrestling

Girls dancing to music

jumping, wrestling, slinging stones and hurling the *javelin*. They practised archery at the butts and fighting with sword and *buckler*. The girls danced with flying feet until the moon rose and they all went home. Many citizens of London delighted in riding out into the country to go hawking or hunting in the parts of Middlesex, Hertfordshire and the Chilterns in which the king had given them the *rights of the chase*. In winter the sport in the fields was to set foaming boars fighting each other

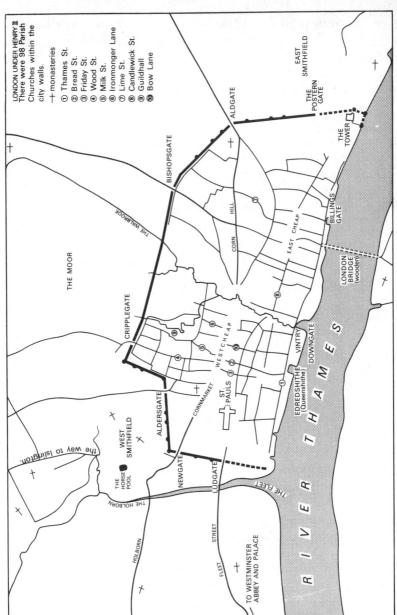

London in the twelfth century

LONDON UNDER HENRY II
There were 98 Parish Churches within the city walls.

+ monasteries

1. Thames St.
2. Bread St.
3. Friday St.
4. Wood St.
5. Milk St.
6. Ironmonger Lane
7. Lime St.
8. Candlewick St.
9. Guildhall
10. Bow Lane

THE MOOR

THE WALBROOK

the way to Islington

WEST SMITHFIELD

THE HORSE POOL

THE HOLBORN

HOLBORN

FLEET STREET

TO WESTMINSTER ABBEY AND PALACE

THE FLEET

LUDGATE

NEWGATE

CORNMARKET

ALDERSGATE

CRIPPLEGATE

ST. PAULS

WESTCHEAP

EDREDSHITHE (Queenshithe)

VINTRY

DOWNGATE

LONDON BRIDGE (wooden)

BILLINGS GATE

EAST CHEAP

CORN HILL

BISHOPSGATE

ALDGATE

EAST SMITHFIELD

THE POSTERN GATE

THE TOWER

RIVER THAMES

Hunting

with their terrible tusks, or baiting bulls or bears by setting packs of hounds loose on them. The favourite winter sport came when the great marsh outside the city wall on the north (the part we now call Moorfields) was frozen over. Then swarms of young men went out to play games on the ice:

Some, gaining speed in their run, with feet set well apart, slide sideways over a vast expanse of ice. Others make seats out of a large lump of ice and whilst one sits thereon, others with linked hands run before and drag him along behind them. So swift is their sliding that sometimes their feet slip and they all fall on their faces. Others, more skilled at winter sports, put on their feet the shin-bones of animals, binding them firmly round their ankles and, holding poles shod with iron in their hands, which they strike from time to time against the ice, they are propelled swift as a bird in flight. Sometimes two of them run against each other in this way from a great distance, and, lifting their poles, each tilts against the other.

Fitz-Stephen thought London was a splendid city. He only found two things wrong with it: the people were gluttonous, eating and drinking far too much, and there were too many fires which swept through the wooden houses, licking up the thatched roofs and sometimes burning down whole streets in one night. King Henry might have added a third bad thing: too many violent tempers among the citizens which led to street fights and murders. All the same, he was probably proud of his great capital and it was very useful, for he gained much money from its wealth.

9 King Henry with his Family and Friends

Henry was a strong ruler. His servants feared and usually obeyed him; barons and others who went against his will found themselves severely punished. Did he get his own way all the time? So often powerful kings have a weak spot and perhaps Henry's was his violent temper. When he was in a rage he could say and do things which, when he was calm, his good sense would have told him were stupid. We are all apt to lose our tempers with the people nearest to us and Henry found his family more difficult to manage than his kingdom. He also lost his temper badly with the man who had been his close friend – Thomas Becket. Because of mistakes he made with his family and his friend, Henry was not able to get his own way entirely.

Henry married a very famous wife. She had been Eleanor, Duchess of Aquitaine, a young and beautiful heiress, possessing

These two carved heads at Langon (France) may be Henry and Eleanor

great wealth of lands in Aquitaine and Poitou. You can find these on the map on p. 20. At fifteen she had been married to Louis VII and had become the queen of France. But the marriage did not work well and finally they were divorced. When she was twenty-nine she met for the first time the young Henry (then eighteen) who was to become King Henry II. They were married while he was still duke of Normandy but soon, when King Stephen died, she became queen of England.

Boats crossing the Channel

She and Henry crossed the Channel in a terrible storm but they reached London safely. Queen Eleanor at first made Henry's court a splendid and exciting place, full of the colour of rich clothes and the poetry of troubadours. Poor young men who looked handsome, could sing and could write poetry came to her court to try and make their fortune. They wrote poems on her beauty and charm, on the flowers of summertime and the white swans on the river. In the evenings they entertained the court with stories of lovers like Tristan and Isolde, or of fierce battles and the valiant deeds of knights. One of these troubadours, named Bernard, wrote many poems about Eleanor. Here are a few lines from one of them: 69

When the sweet breeze
Blows hither from your dwelling
Methinks I feel
A breath of paradise.

At first Eleanor helped Henry in the work of governing all his vast lands (some of them really hers). Sometimes she held a royal court and did justice on her own. She put her own seal on important papers and had her own income to pay for her own household. Soon she began to have a large family. The first one, William, died young. But then in quick succession there came Henry, Matilda, Richard, Geoffrey, Eleanor, Joanna and John. All these babies must have taken much of her attention. Eleanor was a strongminded woman who liked to go her own way and especially she liked her own court where she could surround herself with graceful young courtiers who flattered her. Perhaps also she got bored with Henry's perpetual travelling. So the king and queen began to grow apart.

In the meantime Henry had found a friend in a clever Londoner, Thomas Becket, who had been educated in the Archbishop of Canterbury's court and in 1155 became the king's Chancellor. Henry and he made a good pair, hunting and hawking together, but governing the country together just as energetically. Henry trusted Thomas and often left him to do some of the work of government. Thomas became the most important man in the kingdom after the king. He wore rich clothes and had a splendid train of servants. His grand house in London was full of people coming to ask favours and some people said that he gave his guests better dinners than the king did. When Henry wanted to send a special messenger to the king of France, he chose Thomas Becket who rode to Paris with such a rich cavalcade that every one was astonished. When Henry wished to make sure that the barons of England would be faithful to his heir if he himself were to die, he sent Thomas back to England from France with the little Henry, aged seven, in his care. Thomas called all the barons together at Winchester

and there he put a small gold crown on the little boy's head, while all the barons and bishops knelt to swear fealty to him. Henry thought he had a most faithful friend in Thomas, one who would stand by himself and his family in all danger.

But just at this moment the Archbishop of Canterbury died and, as we have seen, Henry had the idea of making Becket the new archbishop so that he could be sure that the Church would do as he, the king, willed. When the king told Becket what he meant to do, Thomas jokingly touched his own rich, embroidered sleeve, saying that this was not fit for a churchman. More seriously, he warned the king that things would not go as Henry meant, for the two of them would certainly quarrel. Henry got his way and Thomas Becket was consecrated as Archbishop of Canterbury, but it turned out exactly as Thomas had foretold. The new archbishop resigned his office as the king's chancellor, began to live like a sober churchman and put the needs of the Church first – even before what the king wanted. Henry tried at first to be moderate but he could not bear the thought that Thomas would no longer do just as he willed. He began to lose his temper, to do mean things to his archbishop, to get in a state of rage where he could not think sensibly. So a violent quarrel began between the two one-time friends. Becket was obstinate and aggravating; Henry full of

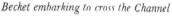

Becket embarking to cross the Channel

hate. The archbishop finally escaped across the Channel from England and took refuge outside the king's dominions. The Pope and various other people tried to end the quarrel. Once Henry and Thomas were persuaded to meet and make it up: they gave each other the kiss of peace but each knew that the quarrel was not over. It ended in disaster. Becket, back in Canterbury, once again refused to obey the king's wishes and Henry, in France, burst into a wild rage when he heard the news.

Becket parting in anger from King Henry and King Louis

I expect you know the rest of the story: how the king exclaimed: 'My subjects are *sluggards*; they allow me to be made the laughing-stock of a low-born clerk'; how four of his courtiers jumped on their horses, rode off, crossed the sea and came to Canterbury; how they murdered Becket there in the cathedral. Henry had apparently got his way, for Becket was dead, but the murder put the king so much in the wrong that he must often have wished he had not spoken in anger.

One of the last disputes between Becket and Henry had been about the crowning of the king's heir. Henry's family of sons was now growing up. They were fine, energetic boys and they wanted lands of their own to rule. Henry's great problem was whether to hand over to his elder sons any of the vast lands he ruled, and, if so, whether to let them govern these lands themselves. You might think that he would be glad not to have to journey continually round so many places and keep his eye on so many people at once, but Henry loved power and did not want to give up one little bit of it anywhere. Perhaps also he wondered whether his sons would take as much trouble to govern well as he did. When the heir to his throne, the young Henry, was fourteen, King Henry announced that his heir would have Maine and Anjou in France, as well being one day King of England. The next, Richard – a tough boy with bold darting eyes and long arms – was his mother's favourite and she declared that he was to have her lands of Poitou and Aquitaine. The third, Geoffrey, then only nine years old, was made Count of Brittany. The baby John got nothing.

Perhaps the boys thought that they would get some of their lands at once and start on an exciting life. But nothing happened. Their father went on governing and they were still kept under tutors, learning good manners as well as how to fight on horseback. But King Henry soon needed to do something more about his heir, for he was determined that there should be no dispute about the crown, if he were suddenly killed, as there

Crowning the young king and feasting him afterwards. The old king serves the young one.

had been in the days of King Stephen. You will remember that years before, when Becket was still the king's friend, he had made the barons swear to be faithful to the little Henry. But now King Henry wanted much stronger promises from his chief nobles. So in 1170 he had his son solemnly crowned in Westminster Abbey and feasted with great splendour. All the chief men did homage to the young king and the old king thought he had got his way. There had been great difficulty over this coronation. Becket, as Archbishop of Canterbury, should have performed it, but this time he refused to help the king. Henry made the Archbishop of York do it instead and this brought on the last quarrel with Becket which led to his death.

Soon Henry was in trouble with his family. Queen Eleanor no longer lived with her husband. Perhaps this was because he had a beautiful young girl called Rosamond – rose of the world – for whom he built a bower at Woodstock. But Eleanor

This picture shows the kind of clothes Eleanor would wear and the chair she might sit in

also left the king because she liked power of her own. She went back to her own lands of Poitou and Aquitaine and settled down at Poitiers to rule as duchess. This meant that as the sons grew up they could turn to their mother for help against their father. Henry saw trouble coming from these boys. One of the writers of the time, Gerald of Wales, tells a story about a picture that Henry had painted on a wall in his palace at Westminster. It showed a great eagle with wings wide-spread, being attacked by four young eaglets. 'I am the eagle,' said Henry, 'and the young ones are my four sons. They will pursue me till I die.' And Gerald adds: 'A man's enemies are in his own house.'

Soon Henry heard that a rebellion of his sons was brewing. The three elder ones were annoyed because Henry had taken away some lands and castles from them to give to the youngest brother, John, when a marriage was arranged for him. Queen Eleanor in her court at Poitiers egged on her rebellious sons. The plan was to get the French King Louis – Henry's enemy – to help them against their father. King Henry tried to stop this: he crossed to France and insisted on taking the young Henry off on a hunting expedition with him. But one night when he was deeply asleep the young man escaped from his father's bed-chamber, slipped out of the castle and rode off to Paris. This was the start of a rebellion that frightened the old Henry. Louis of France declared him to be no longer king of England and tried to put the young Henry in his place. Crowds of discontented people flocked to join the sons of Henry. They were young and handsome. Henry was the beauty and flower of all Christian princes, said his devoted servant, William the Marshal. Richard was as strong as a hammer, said Gerald of Wales. Geoffrey was clever and cunning, as swift as lightning, men said. Their father might well be afraid. But the old king had experienced, loyal servants, more money, and therefore more soldiers. In the hot summer months he crushed the rebellion, brought fire and ruin to Poitou and captured Queen Eleanor as she was trying to escape, dressed as a man. He took her back to England as a prisoner.

For the rest of his life the old Henry never felt safe with his family. He managed for years to keep the young Henry from again rebelling openly, but he was bitter and discontented because his father never let him be a real king. He was jealous of Richard, who was allowed to rule in Poitou and Aquitaine and was successful in conquering rebel barons. The three elder brothers were all suspicious of what their father might give to

75

F

Henry's sons quarrelling at court might have looked like this

the youngest, John. But they were always quarrelling among themselves as well. Geoffrey, the third brother, said: 'Do you not know that no one of us loves another, but that always, brother against brother, and son against father, we try our utmost to injure each other?' While the brothers were divided, the old king managed to prevent rebellion. But when Henry and Richard actually started fighting each other, the old Henry tried to stop it. In the midst of his trouble the young Henry suddenly got a fever and died at the age of twenty-eight. His father was broken-hearted, for although his heir had been such a problem to him, the old king loved him greatly.

Richard was now Henry's heir, but he was no easier to manage. In the very last year of old Henry's life Richard joined with the French king, now Philip Augustus, in a fight against his father. Geoffrey was against him too and finally even John slipped off to join the rebels. Henry was too old to fight as fiercely as he once could. He had spent long years riding furiously from one part of his dominions to another, crossing the Channel in lashing storms, fighting battles and besieging castles, watching everyone and keeping his finger on the government. He had never had any rest and now he was worn out. At one point in the last fight Richard very nearly captured his own father. Finally, the old king fell ill. Philip Augustus and Richard

Eleanor and her son Richard both outlived Henry and were buried side by side

forced him to give up lands and make promises that he had fought hard not to do. He grew worse and died, with none of his family near him. It was the year 1189.

So the great and powerful Henry, with so strong a will and such strength to see that it was obeyed, was finally defeated by his own family. He did not get his way always. But although he failed to manage his family, he built in England a wonderful plan of government through which his servants could enforce his will, even when he was overseas. On the whole the king's will was used on the side of good law and justice, so that violent deeds were punished, weak people were protected from bullying people, and royal servants who cheated were found out and punished. The next king, Richard I, was very different from his father, much more fond of fighting than of governing. But Henry's methods of government were so strong and firm that 77 his servants could go on ruling England in the same way while Richard went on a crusade and fought in France. With some changes, the same rules of government went on while Richard and John were kings of England. Henry II made England the best governed country in western Europe. He also taught the English people to manage much of the business of government for themselves. They had to catch and bring criminals to justice, answer questions about rights to land, assess their neighbours' wealth and collect fines and taxes. It was 'self-government at the king's command.'

Like all kings Henry got nothing out of it in the end. He was buried in the abbey at Fontevrault and this was the *epitaph* on his tomb

I am Henry the King, to me
Divers realms were subject.
I was duke and count of many provinces.
Eight feet of ground is now enough for me
Whom many kingdoms failed to satisfy.

Henry II's tomb at Fontevrault

How Do We Know?

It is not at all easy to find out exactly how a medieval king managed his kingdom. Day-to-day government is not as exciting as battles, sieges of castles, royal marriages, crusades, big quarrels and the deaths of important people. Most medieval chroniclers preferred to tell about these things rather than about the way the king did ordinary business. But we are lucky in England because English writers began to be interested in the way government worked before almost anyone else in western Europe. So, as you know, Richard the Treasurer wrote his Dialogue of the Exchequer telling us so exactly about the way the king's accounts were done that we can almost imagine ourselves to be there. Even before this, in the time of Henry I, someone had written down an account of how the king's household worked, called the 'Constitutio Domus Regis'. One of Henry II's servants, perhaps his Justiciar, Ranulf Glanville, wrote a book about law and justice which describes for us some of Henry's new methods. There were other men around the king who were interested in the new ways of doing justice. They got hold of copies of the king's orders to put in their chronicles and took trouble to describe meetings of the king's council when these changes were discussed. Two writers who tell us a lot are Ralph de Diceto, dean of St Paul's, and Roger Howden who wrote a chronicle which in its first form was by accident put under a false name, Benedict of Peterborough.

Today, if we were studying how government is done, we should find miles and miles of government records stating for many different departments exactly what had been decided in thousands of matters. In Henry II's time government servants were only just beginning to realise the need to keep a record, so that you could turn back and see exactly what had been done or agreed. The first business in which they saw an urgent need to keep a record was that of the king's money – his income and expenses. I expect you will quickly see why a money account was the most urgent. The pipe rolls are the first set of government records we have. We do not know just when they were started, but it was probably in the reign of Henry I, since we have one pipe roll belonging to his reign. Perhaps others have been lost. From Henry II's time onwards we have a continuous series of pipe rolls which tell us an enormous amount about the way English kings received and spent their money. We also have some of the actual tallies used in the Exchequer. Many of these were nearly burnt as useless but were just saved in time. Other government records started a little later, some in the reign of King John. So for Henry II's ways of doing justice we have to rely mostly on what Glanville tells us.

For London we are very lucky, for no one else described a city of this time in such detail as Fitz-Stephen gives us in his description of London. Of course he tells us most about what interested him most. Obviously he was very keen on sport. If you wanted to know about some things in London, for example, its churches, you might be disappointed with Fitz-Stephen. That is the way with historical sources: we can only have what writers at the time thought worth writing about. That is why we know so much about Queen Eleanor and Henry's sons, as well as about the king's quarrel with Becket. These things excited people and so they told the whole story very fully. Our chief problem in using these stories is that people took sides in the quarrels and, as you know, two accounts of one quarrel can often be quite different if told from opposite sides.

All these writings are in Latin, the language in which most people wrote in those days. But many have been translated into English. You will find large parts of them translated in one fat book: 'English Historical Documents', volume 2, edited by D. C. Douglas and published by Eyre and Spottiswoode. You will have to use the Table of Contents at the beginning of the book carefully to pick out what you want.

Things to Do

1 Class Project: Write and act two scenes on the sheriff at the Exchequer (a) in the Lower Exchequer (b) in the Upper Exchequer. You can invent a lot of imaginary business and argument about it. You might pretend the sheriff is the one from your own county and put in local names and places.

Afterwards discuss these points:

Could you invent better ways of keeping a check on the sheriff?

Was it really necessary to have all those officials present at a meeting of the Exchequer?

Why did the king not simply take as much money as he could from the people without bothering about what was right and lawful?

2 Find out about the history of the jury after Henry II's time. Have a class discussion on trial by battle, trial by ordeal and trial by jury. Why did trial by a jury which gave a verdict of guilty or innocent finally take the place of ordeal or battle as a way of deciding a case?

3 If you can, visit a law court to hear some cases. Then make a list of the most important points necessary for good justice (or fair play, as you might call it).

4 Another subject for class discussion: Has the prime minister of England today less or more freedom to govern as he likes than King Henry II in the twelfth century?

5 What kinds of taxes do we have today? Make two lists, one of present taxes and one of Henry II's taxes. Study the differences.

6 Some ideas for writing:

(a) Imagine yourself a servant in the king's household in the twelfth century – you could choose to be the cook, the washerwoman, the keeper of the bath, or whichever of the servants you fancied; write an account of King Henry as you see him.

(b) Write a letter from Richard of Anesti (see p. 50) to the king complaining about all the trouble he is having in getting his case heard.

(c) Write a letter from one of Henry's sons to his father demanding more power.

(*d*) Write a poem by a troubadour for Queen Eleanor.

7 Some ideas for painting:

(*a*) The procession of all the king's household and baggage on the road (see pp. 14–15)

(*b*) The king holding court in Westminster Hall (see p. 51)

(*c*) The sports of London (see pp. 63–67)

8 Read the description of horses on p. 63. Make drawings of them. Watch any horses you can see to find out whether they walk and trot in the way Fitz-Stephen says.

9 Some ideas for handwork:

(*a*) Make a model of the Upper Exchequer with puppet figures round the table.

(*b*) Try cutting some tallies for yourself.

(*c*) Make some figures and dress them in the various sorts of armour required by the Assize of Arms (see p. 45).

Glossary

to *abjure the realm*, to swear to leave the country for ever

assay, test to see if a metal (here silver) is mixed with other metals

assize, set of rules made by the king (it has other meanings too)

aubergel, tunic of chain mail to protect a fighter but less costly than the hauberk (see below)

buckler, shield

bullion, silver or gold metal before it is turned into coins

carette, small cart

chamberlain, official who looks after the king's bedchamber

Chancellor, official who keeps the king's Great Seal

charger, large war-horse

charter, important document in which king or baron made promises or gave gifts in writing

chattels, possessions

circuit, journey of the king's justices round part of the country

civil justice, disputes between people which were brought to the king's court to be judged

criminal justice, cases of serious crime (murder, robbery etc.)

dapifer, official who looked after the king's household

to *dispense*, to give out supplies (food or drink)

disseisin, turning someone out of his house or land

Domus Regis, latin for King's House

epitaph, words written when someone is dead, often put on his grave

erasure, a crossing out or scratching out of words already written

escheat, land which has come back to the king, perhaps because a baron has forfeited it for doing wrong

Exchequer, King's Treasury and Accounts Department

to *execute a writ*, to do what the king commands in a letter

eyre, journey

falconer, man who looks after a kind of hawk called a *falcon*

farm, many small rents and payments put together in one lump sum to be paid

fuller, craftsman who thickened cloth by trampling it in water

gimlet, sharp tool for piercing

guild, company of workers in one craft who banded together

hauberk, tunic of chain mail to protect a fighter

headpiece of iron, rough kind of helmet

hundred, one of the districts into which counties were divided

husbandry, farming

incorruptible, not persuadable by bribes to give what you believe to be a wrong judgment

inquest, inquiry

javelin, short spear which you hurled at the enemy

jury of accusation, group of men (often twelve) whose duty was to accuse people suspected of crimes

Justiciar, king's chief official for doing justice; sometimes he acted in the place of the king in his absence

mark, a coin worth about 13s 4d

Marshal, official who looked after the king's court outside his private rooms, organising ceremonies, processions and public occasions

mercenary, paid soldier

militia, ordinary people who had to carry weapons and train for fighting without pay

minstrel, musician who plays an instrument and/or sings

palfrey, small horse suitable for ladies to ride

petition, request made in writing

quilted doublet, thick padded jacket or tunic which protected the wearer when fighting

reeve, official who manages farm arrangements in a village

relief, sum of money paid by an heir for the right to have land which he had inherited

representative, someone who speaks for a whole group of people

rights of the chase, right to hunt and to hawk

scutage, money paid instead of going to fight for the king

sergeaunty, grant of land in return for special services

sheriff, king's official at the head of the county or shire (his name means shire-reeve)

sluggard, very lazy person

stud, establishment where horses are kept

sumpter-horse, horse for carrying baggage

surety, someone who promises to see that an accused man comes to court

swine, pigs

tally, receipt for money, cut on a piece of wood
tithing, about ten men grouped together to help with law and order
tourn, court held by the sheriff in each hundred
tremulous, trembling or quivering with excitement
troubadour, poet who sang his poems
usher, servant who announces people formally and brings them into
 court
vintner, wine merchant
writ, letter written in the king's name